Winning God's Heart:
A Biblical Path to Intimate Friendship with God

Winning God's Heart: A Biblical Path to Intimate Friendship with God

Published by 1:11 Publishing
An imprint of Little Dozen Press
Crystal Beach, ON, Canada
littledozen.com

Copyright © 2018 by Carolyn Currey

For bulk order information or for more information about 1:11 Ministries, visit one11ministries.com.

Unless otherwise noted, all Scripture quotations are taken from the Holman Christian Standard Bible®, Copyright © 1999, 2000, 2002, 2003, 2009 by Holman Bible Publishers. Used by permission. Holman Christian Standard Bible®, Holman CSB®, and HCSB® are federally registered trademarks of Holman Bible Publishers.

Scriptures marked "ESV" are taken from The ESV® Bible (The Holy Bible, English Standard Version®). ESV® Text Edition: 2016. Copyright © 2001 by Crossway, a publishing ministry of Good News Publishers. The ESV® text has been reproduced in cooperation with and by permission of Good News Publishers. Unauthorized reproduction of this publication is prohibited. All rights reserved.

Scriptures marked "GNT" are taken from the Good News Translation® (Today's English Version, Second Edition). Copyright © 1992 American Bible Society. All rights reserved.

Scriptures marked "NIV" is taken from THE HOLY BIBLE, NEW INTERNATIONAL VERSION®, NIV® Copyright © 1973, 1978, 1984, 2011 by Biblica, Inc.® Used by permission. All rights reserved worldwide.

Scriptures marked "NASB" taken from the New American Standard Bible® (NASB), Copyright © 1960, 1962, 1963, 1968, 1971, 1972, 1973, 1975, 1977, 1995 by The Lockman Foundation. Used by permission. www.Lockman.org

All Rights Reserved. This book, or any portion thereof, may not be reproduced or transmitted in any form or by any means, electronic or mechanical, including photocopying, recording, or by an information storage and retrieval system (except by a reviewer, who may quote brief passages in a review or other endorsement, or in a recommendation to be printed in a magazine, newspaper, or on the Internet) without written permission from the publisher.

ISBN: 978-1-927658-47-5

Winning God's Heart

By Carolyn Currey

Table of Contents

Winning God's Heart	7
Abraham	9
Moses	27
David	49
Matthew	69
John	79
Mary of Bethany	93
My Story	107
Your Story	121

WINNING GOD'S HEART

The bright red letters on the book spine were eye-catching. At four, I had just learned to read, and the unlocked world of words was a constant playground. I slowly sounded out the title: *Flirting . . . with . . . the Devil.*

"Mommy, what does *flirting* mean?"

My mother handled the question well. "It means trying to get someone's attention."

I thought on that for a minute. Clearly this was a stupid title. What a waste of time it would be to try to get the devil's attention!

"Mommy, I will NOT flirt with the devil," I informed her. "I will flirt with God."

The Bible lets us know that God is interested in relationship with us. Within the context of his open invitation to humanity, it is indeed possible to "catch his attention" in a special way and embark on an adventure of mutual response. In fact, it's possible to go far beyond flirting and build a deep, intimate, and lasting relationship with God as we win his heart and he wins ours.

At four years old I didn't know how that could be done, but I was beginning a lifelong journey to find out.

ABRAHAM

The record of those who have won God's heart begins with a man in a tent. An elderly man with a wife who couldn't give him children. He didn't stand out in any way. In fact, at the advanced age of seventy-five he was still doing whatever his dad, Terah, told him to do. Terah decided to head down toward Canaan, and the records say that he took his son Abram and daughter-in-law Sarai, packed up and headed out. They never reached Canaan but settled down partway along the road somewhere.

Abram was not anyone of significance. No great deeds. No calling on the name of the Lord. But there was something about him that God liked. Perhaps it was simplicity.

The first record of God's interaction with Abram is very simple. A straightforward command:

> The LORD said to Abram: "Go out from your land, your relatives, and your father's house to the land that I will show you." . . . So Abram went, as the LORD had told him. (Genesis 12:1, 4)

That was all. The Lord said. Abram did. No questions, no fleeces, no excuses. Not even a conversation about how this would work or where he was going. He just went. Apparently his allegiance, obedience, and trust were already fixed long before God called him to go. Simple trust followed by straightforward obedience wins the heart of God.

> Then the LORD appeared to Abram and said, "I will give this land to your offspring." So he built an altar there to the LORD who had appeared to him. (Genesis 12:7)

Once again that fascinating lack of questions.

Abram doesn't have kids. His wife is already too old. But when God says Abram's children will have the land, Abram doesn't argue or question. He builds an altar.

Building an altar was a sign that something of significance had occurred in that place. So God says a woman already sixty-five years old will have a child, and Abram makes a big pile of rocks to say, "You are God. I honor what you have said. I will not forget what you've promised me."

At this point Abram is just listening. He can't know much about God; there has been very little divine revelation to this point, and his family has worshipped whatever local deity seemed convenient. But he's responding to God's authority in obedience. He's responding to God's promises with honor and trust. He's not demanding that God get moving and prove himself. He's taking God at face value, believing that God is as God declares himself to be, and responding on the basis of that. Abram's humility gives him a shortcut to God's heart. God doesn't have to spend years convincing Abram of his trustworthiness, his power, his heart of love toward Abram. They're just getting down to business. God says, Abram does. God promises, Abram believes.

Lack of doubt is attractive to God. Doubt was the original foothold of sin on earth. Eve listened to the serpent whispering, "Did God really say?", and she acted on that doubt rather than on what she knew of God's character. The "did God really say" attitude is an affront to God. It puts up unnecessary walls and roadblocks, where well-placed hope would make the journey easy.

Abram did not respond with a serpent's doubting heart. He evidenced plain hope and simply believed that God would follow through on his promises.

Hundreds of years later, Abram ended up in the "hall of fame" in the book of Hebrews. Hebrews 11 says, "Now faith is the reality of what is hoped for, the proof of what is not seen. For our ancestors won God's approval by it" (Hebrews 11:1–2).

If nothing else, right at the beginning of their relationship, Abram won God's approval by his hope. But that's only the start. After all, what kind of a relationship is it when the parties simply *approve* of each other?

So far God has been the one to seek out Abram. He has initiated the conversations. Now Abram takes his own step. When he stopped his journey between the towns of Ai and Bethel, Genesis says, "He built an altar to Yahweh there, and he called on the name of Yahweh" (Genesis 12:8).

Ai means "the ruin." *Bethel* means "house of God." Abram stands between them and takes the initiative to call on God himself. He is somewhere in the middle, just doing life. He's not in a ruin, nor is he standing in the house of God. There has been no major disaster, no big revelation. In this moment, he's just trudging through the sand, one day after another. But he takes this mundane moment, this in-between moment, to call on God. To call on his name. To align himself under his authority.

Those moments can seem like nothing to us. Washing dishes and calling on God. Praying in a car. On a walk. While clocking out of work. No major problems, no major blessings. No big reason to need God's help, no seemingly big reason to thank him. These are the moments when we tend to ignore God, because why would he even be interested—and frankly, why would we put in the time when there's no big thing to deal with and a million small things to capture our attention?

But it is here that Abram makes the choice to affirm that he is aligned with God. And like before, he makes an altar to say this moment is important. The mundane and the ordinary are important. Asking God to be in those moments, those everyday life moments, is life changing.

Time goes by, and Abram starts to wonder about God's promises. He took God at face value at first, but so far there's no land and no son. So he reminds God of his unfulfilled promise: "Look, you have given me no offspring, so a slave born in my house will be my heir" (Genesis 15:3).

Although God is not fond of doubt, he doesn't have a problem with Abram's questions. He knows Abram doesn't have much to go on. It's not like he can sit down with a Bible and half a dozen biographies containing stirring accounts of God's faithfulness through the ages. He has no proof of the future or history of the past. So when the promises don't show and Abram questions, God is ready to give assurance where there is none. He simply states that the slave won't inherit Abram's goods; the promised son will. He doesn't give times, dates, or explanations. He just says it like it is, giving the reassurance Abram needs.

Abram's response is famous: "Abram believed the LORD, and he credited it to him as righteousness" (Genesis 15:6). Once again, that simplicity. Nothing external had changed. But that wasn't necessary to keep Abram's hope alive.

Any believer knows that God loves righteousness. Generally when we think of righteousness, we think of doing good things. Sending money to feed starving children in Africa. Not yelling back at the irritating relative. Paying your taxes and not cheating. Helping out at the church. All this stuff is good, but we've missed the point somewhere along the way. Righteousness applies to how you handle your situation, whatever it may be. Abram didn't do. He just believed. And God said that was righteousness. Righteousness was nothing more than Abram affirming God's character as faithful and aligning his own life with it, staking all his hope on God's faithfulness.

God decides what righteousness looks like. It's worth asking what righteousness looks like in your circumstances right now. The answer may be surprising, because God wants relationship far more than he wants acts of service.

I'm really good at the hurry-up-and-do-all-the-things gig. My list is always long, and there's never enough time to get it all done. When I look at it, it's all good stuff! It's all directed toward advancing the kingdom of God, and yet the King doesn't seem nearly as interested in my list as he does in spending time with me. As a dancer and co-director of a performing arts ministry, I'll fill my day with production details, choreography, rehearsals, tour promotion, writing, and travel plans. But when I stop and listen, he's saying, "Come sit by the water with me for a little while and leave the work behind."

Whenever I answer that beckoning voice, I'm reminded of how much more fulfilling the time with him is. It's almost a surprise every time. We talk about things that have nothing to do with the workday that a moment ago seemed so pressing. I trust him with all-the-things and give him the time he wants. It turns out that time is exactly what I need, and for some reason, me leaving my list to have a chat pleases him. He calls it righteousness. Seeking him first. Not the list. Just him.

It's not that I never get any work done. But God himself is the priority. Some time ago he told me, "Don't fill every hour of your day just so you can feel busy and accomplished. Busy is not equal to righteous." In our overworked society, being busy all the time seems important. If you're not run off your feet, you don't have a life. It's time to shift the culture. It's time to move our identities back toward who we are and not what we do.

Abram allowed himself to be defined by his relationship with God, giving him an unusual identity for his time. While his contemporaries bowed to idols or tried to appease unknown deities, Abram spoke with God. God was known to him. Abram talked with God about his descendants, who didn't exist yet. He and the Lord had conversations about things that would happen hundreds of years later. He accepted the new name God gave him—*Abraham*—and was known by it for the rest of his life. He made dinner for God and a couple of angels: bread and butter, milk and meat. He was called a friend of God (James 2:23). He even negotiated with God.

Abraham's negotiating story, found in Genesis

18, has some fascinating moments. He's just served dinner to God, who has reconfirmed the promise of a son for Abraham. Now he's walking with his guests, three men who are not mere men, on the road to Sodom. So far nothing has been said or asked about their business. But it seems God can't keep it to himself any longer.

> Then the LORD said, "Should I hide what I am about to do from Abraham?" (Genesis 18:17)

The answer to God's question was no. God *wanted* to talk with Abraham about what he was doing. Think about this for a moment. God has things on his heart—things he's doing in your neighbourhood, your city, your country. He doesn't want to do them on his own, and often he won't. Psalm 115 says, "The heavens are the LORD's, but the earth He has given to the human race" (Psalm 115:16). When God gave us authority over the earth, he desired partnership with us in governing it. Once again, it comes back to relationship. In working together on something, God adds another layer to his relationship with us. This desire is reflected in his conversation with Abraham.

Sodom has become a really wicked city, God says, and he is on his way to destroy the whole thing. Abraham thinks about this a minute, and since his nephew lives in Sodom, he's concerned. So he negotiates and makes an appeal to God's character.

> Will you really sweep away the righteous with the wicked? . . . You could not possibly do that! Won't the Judge of all the earth do what is just? (Genesis 18: 23, 25)

At this point in his life, Abraham is not on the level of begging God to please do or not do such a thing. He knows God in a more personal way by now, and he is making an appeal based on what he knows about God's nature. He knows him as a supreme ruler but also as a righteous judge. So he essentially asks God to remain true to his character.

The story continues with Abraham negotiating with God to spare Sodom for the sake of fewer and fewer people. The negotiation is never haughty or demanding. Abraham knows who he's talking to, and he gives the respect that's due every step of the way. And God is okay with this. Abraham is exploring the depths of God's mercy, and God wants to be known as merciful. So he has the conversation. Perhaps it is this exploration into unknown territory—a deeper understanding of the character of God—that gives Abraham the trust to face the ultimate test of his life.

When Abraham is one hundred years old, the promised son, Isaac, is born, just as God said. God is proved as faithful. His character is upheld, no matter how impossible the proof must have seemed. But years later, God makes an unthinkable request of Abraham: "'Take your son," he says, "Your only son, Isaac, whom you love, go to the land of Moriah, and offer him there as a burnt offering."

Once again, there is simply silent obedience. As he has done his whole life, Abraham obeys when God speaks. Yet the short conversations in the story show that Abraham still has full confidence in the character of God. He tells his servants to stay at a distance while he and his son go to worship, "Then we will come back to you." His son Isaac asks where the actual sacrifice is, and his father replies that God himself will provide the lamb for the offering. In the face of this incredible test, Abraham never wavers.

Hundreds of years later, we are given some insight into his mind by the book of Hebrews:

> By faith Abraham when he was tested, offered up Isaac. He received the promises and he was offering his unique son, the one it had been said about, "Your seed will be traced through Isaac." He considered God to be able even to raise someone from the dead, and as an illustration, he received him back. (Hebrews 11:17–19)

All the way up the mountain, Abraham is clinging to the promise that his line will continue through Isaac. Isaac has no children yet; therefore today can't be Isaac's day to die. Or at least, to stay dead. Again, remember that Abraham has no history to go on. At this point in history, we have precedent for God raising the dead. In Abraham's time, such a thing had never happened. But Abraham believed that it could and would have to, simply because God is faithful and does not lie. So for God to make good on his promises, Isaac would still have to be alive at the end of the day.

In his willingness to sacrifice his heir, we also see Abraham's priority. Abraham's relationship with God is more important than his relationship with even this loved and long-awaited son. His attitude is one of open-hearted generosity and trust toward God. This is what makes such an incredible relationship possible.

Abraham is not a perfect superhero. He messes up a lot. He lies, and his wife ends up in the local king's harem. Apparently he's okay with that because his own skin is saved. In fact, he pulls that particular trick twice! He doubts God's promises, sleeps with a servant, and tries to help God out by getting a child through her rather than his wife as God had promised. He's human. And yet through it all, Abraham identifies himself as belonging to the Lord. That never wavers. He knows God is involved in his life, and he wants to be in cooperation with that (even when his mode of cooperation is questionable).

When Abraham was called, he had nothing to give except a yes. That was all God was looking for. Abraham was desired by God for his own self, not for anything he could contribute.

Abraham's hope was characterized by action. If he had not believed God, he would not have obeyed everything God told him to do so readily. Some of those things were more than a little outlandish! But the bedrock of his life was that when God said, Abraham did. No question. By his great faith, he left a legacy for many generations.

Abraham was a man after God's heart as much as he could be in his time. Each man and woman following Abraham in walking with God built on that foundation with more passion and extravagance. Abraham was honored because he had little external evidence to go on, little information about the past to tell him God was faithful and worth loving and obeying, yet he sought God wholeheartedly. His was a time of leaning on the character of God—revealed through personal encounter and God's words and promises—above everything else, because there was nothing else.

It isn't God's design that people should walk alone or in isolation. This is why he's placed us into his body, the church, with himself as the head. This has the capacity to be the closest community on earth! However, there is also an element of aloneness in any walk with God. We are each called to a secret relationship with God—one that is cultivated by times alone speaking with him. This takes time, determination, and a willingness to be misunderstood by others.

Those who would outpace their generation in seeking God will often walk alone, simply because they are not satisfied with the status quo. They have run on ahead because they are not satisfied with just a little of God. These people are found throughout the pages of Scripture: Enoch, Noah, Jacob, David, John the Baptist, Paul, and many more. For each one, their life of faith involved an element of walking alone. They were given double honor for their willingness to do this. The same invitation is extended to us. There is so much more to God than you know now. There is so much more available in relationship with him. He has extended the same invitation to you that he extended to Abraham: Come and know him. Come and talk with him. Come and learn his character and faithfulness. Whether you experience this kind of relationship with God will depend on whether you say the simple yes that Abraham did. God says, you do. God promises, you believe. God invites, you run toward him. Nothing complicated is required.

MOSES

Moses. From slave child to Egyptian prince to outcast shepherd to revolutionary, the man himself is often overshadowed by the events surrounding him. Yet Moses was a man who could calm an angry God.

Moses's early story, of a baby in a basket who is rescued by a princess, is well known. Moses grows up in Egypt's court, attempts to become the rescuer of Israel in his own strength, makes Pharaoh really mad, and winds up in the desert herding sheep for forty years. There's no evidence that he seeks God during this time. But just like Abraham, he gets chosen anyway.

Although I speak in this book of catching God's

attention, this is always the reality: God chooses us first. He reaches out to us first. He extends the invitation first, revealing something of himself and drawing us deeper. In Moses's case, God called to him through the means of a burning bush.

A bush burning might not be a rare sight in the desert. After all, it's hot—things sometimes did spontaneously burst into flame out there. But a bush burning, continuing to burn, and suffering no damage—that's different. Moses, at eighty, is apparently still in full command of his senses, including his sense of curiosity. He's not slipped into a superior attitude of "I've seen it all." Perhaps, from God's perspective, this is Moses's first test. He's curious enough to go check out something he doesn't understand. In getting up to go look at a bush, he heads over to unknowingly check out something he understands even less . . . God. When a voice comes from the bush, he realizes his curiosity may have changed the course of his life.

In Moses's first encounter with God, he asks a

question we all ask. God reveals himself to Moses as the God of his fathers Abraham, Isaac, and Jacob, and announces his plan to release the Israelites from their slavery and bring them into the land he promised Abraham hundreds of years ago. Moses is his chosen leader. Moses's current status is outcast shepherd and persona non grata in Egypt, so his question is not surprising: *"Who am I?"*

God's reply has absolutely nothing to do with Moses and absolutely everything to do with what he intends to do for Moses. He promises to be with Moses. Hearing that, Moses responds with a better question: "Well then, who are you?" Or more specifically, "What is your name?"

Up to this point, no one in history has ever asked God his name. Not even Abraham, who was called a friend of God. Moses requests knowledge of God and relational intimacy on a new level, and God responds with the name "I AM."

This is a door to God's heart. A simple request to know more of him can lead to unexpected encounters. Moses just asked for a name so he could introduce God to the leaders of the people. God gave a name: a revelation of himself so that he could be known "in every generation." A request for knowledge and intimacy in a single moment led to a breakthrough for every person who would live after Moses. Do not underestimate the value of asking for more. You are not just asking for yourself.

As the conversation continues, God and Moses get into a realm most of us are more familiar with: testing. The interesting thing is that God offered a sign before Moses ever got around to tests. His ways are different than ours, though. He offered a sign that would only play out after the fact: "This will be the sign to you that I have sent you: when you bring the people out of Egypt, you will all worship God at this mountain" (Exodus 3:12). Simply put, "Trust that it will happen, and when it does, you'll look back and see the proof of it." Not so much the way we want tests to work! God asks us to walk through the doing and then see the proof. We'd rather have the proof before the doing.

"If you really mean it, show me a sign!"

"If you want me to do this, prove it first!"

Boiled down, our objection is simply, "If you want my obedience, prove yourself first." God doesn't have to prove himself. But in his mercy, he often plays the test game with us, especially when we are immature. Even then, however, he hides lessons within the tests. He told Moses to throw his staff on the ground, and it became a snake. Almost certainly a poisonous one, because Moses as a veteran desert shepherd would have known a dangerous snake from a nondangerous one, and he runs from this one. Then God turns the tables: "Pick the snake up by the tail." Anyone who is foolish enough to pick up a snake in the first place knows that one does not do it by the tail. My tomboy sisters used to do this in the backyard with garter snakes, and they got bit until they learned how to grasp a snake correctly: right behind the head where it can't whip around and strike. Moses responds to God and grabs that snake by the tail. This test was his idea; God is testing him back. Moses is learning trust within his own test. And the snake turns into a staff again.

Later, as Moses heads toward Egypt, there is a brief comment made: "And Moses took God's staff in his hand." It's no longer Moses's staff. The encounter has changed the ownership of the object used in the testing. In the same way, when we encounter God and allow him to change us, we change ownership.

> Don't you know that if you offer yourselves to someone as obedient slaves, you are slaves of that one you obey—either of sin leading to death or of obedience leading to righteousness? (Romans 6:16)

Eventually Moses heads back to Egypt, reluctant but obedient. There he faces Pharaoh, popularly known as the god-king and stubborn to the core. Destruction begins to be unleashed as Pharaoh refuses to free the people God has chosen for himself. But as the plagues on Egypt unfold, Moses is watching a double story. With each plague, he sees God's determination to free his people. He gains deeper and deeper glimpses of the heart of God. Yahweh will stop at nothing to bring his people out and woo them to himself. Each strike against their cruel captors is a promise of faithfulness to Israel. By the time they actually walk out of Egypt, they have every reason to trust God and his heart toward them. They have no reason not to commit themselves back to him. Moses, as the message-bearer for all the calamities and the visible deliverer of Israel, has a front-row seat. The signs of God's presence come thick and fast now and cause Moses to return to that original question: "Who are you?"

I find the season in the wilderness the most intriguing part of Moses's life. Finally he leads the Israelites to Mount Sinai, where the whole adventure started with a bush. The Moses who returns to Sinai is not the Moses who finished off the last conversation in this place by whining, "Oh, please send someone else!" He has seen too much. His initial curiosity has grown into hunger. The original sign God promised, "You will worship me at this mountain," has been fulfilled.

The story of Moses's relationship with God can perhaps be summarized in two verses:

> Then Moses brought the people out of the camp to meet God . . . And the people remained standing at a distance as Moses approached the thick darkness where God was. (Exodus 19:17; 20:21)

In the Old Covenant, one could not approach God unless invited to do so. In our day, Jesus is our open invitation: we may come, we may approach God as Moses did. But just as in the past, many will follow their Moses—their pastor, spiritual leader, worship leader, favorite Christian author—out of the camp to meet God . . . and then remain standing at a distance. Sure, there may be darkness where God is. He's unknown, holy, altogether other. We simply don't know what will happen if we approach him. It's not safe. But the alternative is to watch others come close to God while we forever stand at a distance. Isn't it better to get your brave on and move closer?

Some years ago I was finishing a tour with our 1:11 team. I ended up sick just a few days before heading home, and we had to camp out in someone's home for a while. We assumed the fever and sore throat would pass quickly with rest. It didn't. It got worse very quickly, and before long my friends were worried. I wasn't. I'd lapsed into delirium.

I don't know how long I was in that state, but I do remember one incident very clearly. Whether conscious or not, I can't remember, but I saw a curtain in front of me. It was big, and it was swaying a little at one end. My body was at its lowest point, and I could feel my heart working harder and harder. Everything in me felt like it was fighting to keep going, and I didn't dare stop fighting for one minute. Somehow I knew if the curtain moved just a bit further, I'd go behind it and go home for good rather than home to Canada.

I was okay with that, but I also heard God saying firmly, "This is not your time." So I kept willing my heart to beat and my lungs to breathe. That was when I had one of those life-defining moments of clarity. Suddenly nothing mattered anymore except to know and love God. It was like everything I had ever done came up for review, and only what had been done out of love for him mattered. Everything else was like it never existed.

Apart from him saying I wasn't going to die that day, I had no reason to expect that I wouldn't be seeing him face-to-face very soon. And I wanted him. But I also deeply wanted to know him more before I actually saw him. I wanted to be able to take that new understanding and do everything out of love for him.

Clearly, I'm still here. But the wonder of that day has never left me. I know something of what death feels like, and I no longer have any fear of it.

He is there in that valley, and he is fully in charge. But more than that, I am here with a purpose. I want to know him. I want to love him better. I want to push against the unknown, to explore the depths of God I have never dreamed of. I'll be with him forever. There's going to be a wedding. What bride would want to end up at the altar with a man she doesn't know? Would she not want to spend as much time getting to know him and growing in confidence with him before she ended up at the ceremony?

There is no difference between that and our relationship with God. As the Bride of Christ, we will all be at the wedding. Will you be there unsure of the man you marry or delighting in the one you already know?

Moses shared this desire to know God truly and intimately. By the time he reached Sinai the second time, he was hooked. When God calls him up the mountain, he spends forty days and nights there receiving the instruction of God for his people.

Think about that for a moment. Forty days and forty nights on a mountain in the desert listening to God talk. By this time, a serious relationship is underway between God and Moses.

When Moses comes down the mountain, he finds idol worship already springing up among the people. They are worshipping a gold calf made from their gold jewelry, the same jewelry God granted them when he told them how to plunder the Egyptians on their way out. The story is a somber reminder not to worship the gifts he gives us.

God responds with justifiable anger and declares his intention to wipe out these people and form a new nation starting with Moses. In the face of this idolatry and of God's anger, Moses takes it on himself to speak to God. The encounter involves Moses "beseeching" God and God "repenting," changing his mind.

The Hebrew words indicate a closeness that isn't translated into English. "Beseeched" means to be "rubbed or worn." Years ago, I listened to Brother

Andrew preach on this passage. He said, "Moses was so close to God that when God was angry he stroked the face of God."

This kind of closeness is perhaps a little too much for our churchified minds, but what follows fits with that translation. The KJV says that "God repented," but the word used means "to sigh." So Moses strokes the face of God, reminding him of his promises that are based in his very self, begging him to be merciful. And God heaves a deep sigh, knowing how many more times this situation with Israel will play out, and does not destroy them.

Moses doesn't stop there, though. He has a second request.

For many of us, as long as external circumstances are working out, we are happy. If the ministry is well financed, if the career is on track for a promotion, if we are well fed, we are content. Except, of course, for the question in the back of our minds: "Is this all there is to life?" Moses was not prepared to ignore that question.

Initially, God tells him to continue with the project at hand: "Go, leave here, to the land I promised." But there's a catch. "I will not go with you." God promises an angel to go ahead of them and drive out the nations, but they have forfeited his presence. Moses is not okay with this. He heads far out from the camp and sets up a tent. If God will not go with the people, Moses is going where he can find God. The project is not more important than the presence. Even a project promised to be wildly successful and miraculous is not a substitute for the companionship of God. Moses abandons it all until he can get the issue of presence cleared up. It is in this season that one of the most incredible tributes to Moses's life is made:

> The LORD spoke with Moses face to face, just as a man speaks with his friend. (Exodus 33:11)

In this time of laying everything down for the sake of God's presence, Moses gains friendship with

God. Whatever your highest aspirations, whatever ambitions you may hold, they are worth laying completely aside if it means gaining the company of God. Moses's reasons for doing so are found in Exodus 33:15–16:

> "If your presence does not go," Moses responded to Him, "don't make us go up from here. How will it be known that I and Your people have found favor in Your sight unless you go with us? I and Your people will be distinguished by this from all the other people on the face of the earth."

The favour and presence of God are beyond worth. And our desire for this moves God's heart. At Moses's plea, what was a no becomes a yes. Once again God changes his mind because of Moses's request, saying, "I will do this very thing you have asked, for you have found favor in My sight, and I know you by name" (Exodus 33:17).

At this point, a natural response would be,

"Great! Let's get on with our project and take the land!" But this is not Moses's next response. *You see, if the whole point is God's presence, the project is still not the point.* When his presence has been granted, it means you have favor. How are you going to use this favor? You can seek the success of the project, and you will likely succeed. After all, if God's presence and favor are on you, success is a done deal. But you will have cheated yourself and grabbed the thing of second worth. The project is already taken care of. You'll get around to it in good time. In this moment of favor, ask for what really matters.

Moses's immediate response to God's promise of presence is, "Please, let me see your glory." It's not, "Please, let me have the thing." It's, "Please, let me have you." This is the ultimate secret to the heart of God. It's truly putting him first. It's asking for more of him when he lavishes everything else on you. It's counting him of greater worth than his gifts. It's asking for increase when he gives you himself.

God granted Moses's request. He hid him in the cleft of a rock, allowing him to peer out and look at the back of God. Because ultimately, the greatness of God can only be seen in part. We cannot handle the whole thing, but he will give us as much as we can handle. We just have to ask. And keep asking.

The second time God calls Moses up the mountain is a little different. Once again it's forty days and nights. This time it says Moses ate and drank nothing. He is at the point where God is completely enough. When he comes down, he is so full of the glory of God that the Israelites cannot look on his face. What happened between them during that time? There's no detail given in the Scripture, but the encounter is a reminder for those times we think we've seen all there is to God. There's far more than we've yet dreamed of.

Finally God brings his people to the very edge of the promised land. They send in spies, freak out when they see the mighty people of the land, and decide to go back to Egypt. Not surprisingly, God is angry. Once again he is prepared to destroy them and make Moses into a nation instead. And once again, Moses must intercede for the people. It's a little different this time, though. The first time, Moses referenced God's past faithfulness and his covenant with Abraham. This time, Moses is making his appeal based on the very character of God. He's at the point where he is confident enough to appeal based on relationship. It's not a case of "You said this, so please be faithful"; it's "I know you to be unfailing in love, so please be true to your character."

Moses has come a long way from hiding his face at the sight of God. His fear moved first from curiosity to deep desire. Now at last, he moves to confident relationship and an ability to intercede based on what he personally knows of the character of God.

But there is still a point of danger here, even in this place of confidence. It is overconfidence. As it is said: familiarity breeds contempt.

Early in their wanderings, the people wailed for water, and God had Moses strike a rock to bring water out of it for them. Years later, they're in need of water again, and God directs Moses to simply speak to a rock this time. This should be easy by now. God says, Moses does. But perhaps Moses has become overfamiliar. Perhaps he's leaning back on how he's done things before. Perhaps he's losing that curiosity and wonder that led him to check out the bush back at the beginning of this whole crazy adventure. He knows striking the rock worked in the past. Why not stick to the tried and true method?

So that's what he does. Moses has presumed on God, yet God graciously does not allow him to lose face before his people. He brings the water out of the rock, despite Moses's disobedience. But Moses is about to pay a price for his presumption. He has just lost his own entry to the land. As God informs him, he will die just before the people enter it.

On the surface, this may seem like an overreaction on God's part. After all, Moses has worked really hard for God, leading these people through the desert for forty years. Can't God cut him a little slack? Maybe a slightly less harsh punishment? Perhaps that might have worked with someone who knew God less deeply, less intimately, who had less reason to trust. Perhaps the punishment might have been smaller for someone who had not talked with God face-to-face. But Moses was beyond excuse. The relationship between him and God was such that this "small" disobedience constituted complete rebellion, a trashing of everything they had built between them. Moses was essentially throwing God aside and saying he himself was enough. Such an act was worthy of death on the spot *because of the depth of their relationship.*

Beware of this place of complacency. Face-to-face encounters grant you favor. But that favor can be lost. Seeing God's glory does not give you the right to act nonchalant about it. The further you go in his favor, the more carefully you should tread. The more you see of him, the more you should walk in the knowledge that he is altogether holy. Do not assume that because you have favor with God, you are immune from punishment. The closer your relationship is, the more you are held accountable to obedience because of it.

Far from overreacting, God was merciful. He didn't kill Moses on the spot. But he would not let him enter the land. God did, however, give him one last consolation: he promised Moses could look at the land he'd spent forty years journeying toward. When the time came, God and Moses headed up a mountain for a mutual viewing of the promised country. And then Moses died. But even here, the relationship is evident. At the end of his life, God himself buried Moses.

The life of Moses is one of intrigue for us. Throughout the story, one message is clear: There is more to God. It is worth searching out.

DAVID

David the shepherd king is a study in contrasts. He's a picture of what is possible with God and what happens when a leader loses his vision. He's also a study of grace.

We first find David absent. Samuel the prophet has been sent to look over the sons of Jesse to determine which of them will be the next king of Israel. They're lined up for inspection . . . all except the youngest. Apparently no one considered him worth calling in from the sheep. Maybe they just forgot about him. The truth is, they don't know him. They don't know the secret life he leads.

In all his family, no one actually knows what

goes on in the hills with the sheep, David, and God. No one actually knows David or sees his worth. But in those solitary years out in the wilderness, he has been getting to know God and value him. The psalms he wrote out in the hills are the evidence.

> The heavens declare the glory of God,
> and the sky above proclaims his handiwork.
> Day to day pours out speech,
> and night to night reveals knowledge.
> There is no speech, nor are there words,
> whose voice is not heard.
> Their voice goes out through all the earth,
> and their words to the end of the world.
> (Psalm 19:1–4, ESV)

As David learned to know God through creation, he also saw himself as part of that creation, responsible before his Creator:

> Keep back your servant also from presumptuous sins;

> let them not have dominion over me!
> Then I shall be blameless,
> and innocent of great transgression.
> Let the words of my mouth and the meditation of my heart
> be acceptable in your sight,
> O LORD, my rock and my redeemer.
> (Psalm 19:13–14, ESV)

From the very start, David's relationship with God has been one of purity and simplicity. He sees God for who he is, and his desire is to be wholeheartedly in alignment with the righteousness of God.

David has history with God through his predecessors Moses and Abraham. But he has also put in the time to know the character of God for himself. His is a relationship of confidence. He knows God as the Living God. He has taken the time to learn the worth of God, and God responds by affirming David's worth in return. God, in fact, chooses him as the next king of Israel, the one to follow Saul, who is the presently reigning monarch. David is anointed . . . and then sent back to the sheep. He has received the promise, but not the fulfillment.

Nothing seems to have changed, but David takes on the identity of a king from that day. Other people have lots to say about him: conspirator, deserves to die, unknown slave. Even his own brothers call him arrogant and evil-hearted. David never walks in any of those false identities, but only in what God says about him. He knows how to keep his mouth shut and walk in quietness and trust before the One whose opinion really matters.

The defeat of Goliath is the first time we hear David speak. His attitude is one of astonishment and outrage when he hears the giant mocking and threatening the people of Israel: "Just who is this uncircumcised Philistine that he should defy the armies of the living God?" He's astounded that anyone would defy God, and he's confident that God will give him the victory in the situation. To David it's simple: to defy the armies of God is to defy God himself. So the enemy will lose.

In fact, David sees the problem as his responsibility. He is the promised king of Israel. He is already treating Israel as his people, protecting them, and reminding them of who their God is. "All the world will know that Israel has a God," David says, "and this whole assembly will know that it is not by sword or by spear that the LORD saves, for the battle is the LORD's."

David has a rare combination of confidence with humility. His confidence truly is in the Lord, but he never gets uppity or presumptuous about it. His attitude of humility is seen especially throughout the remainder of King Saul's reign. After the defeat of the Philistine giant, David is promoted within the royal courts. When the subject of David's possible marriage to one of Saul's daughters comes up, David doesn't respond like a proud army general—especially not one with a promise of kingship in his future. Instead he says to his fellow servants, "Is it trivial in your sight to become the king's son-in-law? I am a poor man who is common."

Already, David is cultivating in himself the heart of a king by honoring the current king. But not everyone sees it that way. As time goes on, Saul becomes jealous of David and does everything a man can do to make David hate him. David's attitude of honor and respect is never diminished. Forced to go on the run from Saul, more than once he has the chance to kill Saul, take revenge, and seize the promised kingdom by force. He never takes the opportunity. God gave the promise, so God must give the fulfillment. David will not take it in his own way. His attitude is fully expressed in his words to Saul: "May the Lord judge between you and me, and may the Lord take vengeance on you for me, but my hand will never be against you."

David is experiencing one of the hardest tests God gives to those he wants to raise up: he is being trained in the crucible of honor. In the midst of an unfair situation, will you choose to honor those to whom honor is positionally due, even when they seem to have personally forfeited the right to be honored? Will you allow God to mold the heart of royalty within you, even when the way is painful? It is much easier to take the way of a slave and get your own revenge. The identity is yours to choose.

If you walk with a slave mentality, you will not believe that anything rightly belongs to you. You will not know that you are an heir, and that you have a family protecting you and watching your back. As a result you will sneak around, backbite, and grasp for whatever can be gained. But if you live with the mindset of royalty, you will refuse to lower yourself to behave in a shameful way, even though you are being treated shamefully. You will know that such behavior is beneath you, not because you are high and mighty but because you are a child of the King.

I know someone who was painfully betrayed by a friend. In that situation, she realized that the betrayal she had experienced had been passed down from one person to another for quite some time. She was next in the receiving line because no one before her had chosen to behave differently. As she prayed about it, she realized she could make a choice based out of an identity of royalty in that situation and cause the cycle of betrayal to stop with her. If she didn't hang onto the hurt and act it out by betraying someone else, the line would end. She chose forgiveness. The line of betrayal and pain ended with her.

There's a line in the movie *Ever After* I love that encapsulates this concept: "You have been born to privilege, and with that comes specific obligation."

As the children of God, when we are born into his kingdom, we are born to privilege. We are reborn into a royal line. Royalty behaves in certain ways. A royal family has protocol, expectations, a higher standard. In God's royal family, the standards are even higher. There is obligation to love, not just outwardly but completely from the heart. This is noblesse oblige in its highest form. When we are treated badly by others, as children of God we have a standard of love and honor to uphold. It's what Jesus did. As his brothers and sisters, we can do no less.

David submits to this training for many years before he ever sees the fulfillment of the promise. His humility is apparent throughout, even in the moments when he needs a course correction. The story of the fool and his wise wife is one such situation.

As David and his men are out in the wilderness, they meet up with the shepherds of Nabal, a local rich man. His flocks are extensive, and David takes it upon himself to protect the shepherds in the wilderness. As they later report to Nabal, "The men treated us well. When we were in the field, we weren't harassed and nothing of ours was missing the whole time we were living among them. They were a wall around us, both day and night, the entire time we were herding the sheep" (1 Samuel 25:15–16).

After some time, the season for shearing comes around—a traditional time of celebration and bounty. David sends an envoy to Nabal to receive some expected generosity for all he and his men have done for him. Nabal sneers at the men and sends them away with rude remarks and nothing else.

David, understandably, loses his temper: "I guarded everything that belonged to this man in the wilderness for nothing . . . he paid me back evil for good." And in his anger, he heads off to take it out on Nabal and his men.

When Nabal's wife, Abigail, hears the story, she hurries to save her family and pacify David. She takes an attitude of humility and even responsibility for an action she knew nothing about. She also gently reminds David of who he is and how he should be behaving because of his identity as king and child of God:

> The guilt is mine, my lord . . . accept this gift your servant brought to my lord . . . Please forgive your servant's offence, for the LORD is certain to make a lasting dynasty for my lord because he fights the LORD's battles. Throughout your life may evil not be found

in you. When the LORD does for my lord all the good he has promised and appoints you ruler over Israel, there will not be remorse or a troubled conscience for my lord because of needless bloodshed or my lord's revenge. (1 Samuel 25:24, 28, 30)

David stops, thinks, and realizes she's right. At this point, he has a choice. He can uphold his own anger, rights, and status in front of his men and charge on to do what he planned. Undoubtedly, his men are bloodthirsty and ready for action, and it won't be easy to calm them down after he's already riled them up. Or he can calm down, realize that he is in the wrong, accept the gift, and eat lunch. He chooses lunch and wisdom.

"Today," he tells Abigail, "you kept me from participating in bloodshed and avenging myself by my own hand" (1 Samuel 25:33).

David was willing to be corrected. He didn't pigheadedly insist on his own way. Because of his openness to correction, he was able to see God do justice for him. He and his men were wandering in the wilderness, trying to escape King Saul's plan to destroy them all. This was hardly a visible fulfillment of the promise of kingship! On top of that, Nabal was shockingly ungrateful after all David had done for him. But when David stood aside and refused to take revenge into his own hands, God took Nabal down for him. Nabal died within days, and David married Abigail, presumably inheriting all that had been Nabal's. God's justice is thorough, to say the least. In this wilderness season when he was already discouraged, David must have needed this reminder. God was still on his side, and David's job was to let God be God and David not be God.

As he lets God take his rightful place, David learns to seek his face. In fact, during this time in the wilderness, David constantly seeks God's counsel before he steps into any dangerous situation. This is significant, because it shows the role of process in our lives and in the fulfillment of God's promises to us. So often when a promise comes, impatience for fulfillment accompanies it. Instead of waiting on

God's timing, we desire immediate action, and we become frustrated at God in the waiting. In frustration, relationship dies. David doesn't do this. He keeps a constant relationship going by seeking God's will for each situation out there in the desert. His story is reminiscent of Abraham, in that God speaks and David does. But David is taking it a step further. Each time he seeks God for counsel, he is initiating the connection. He's taking responsibility to build a strong bond with God.

One story in particular stands out as an example of David's commitment to obedience. He is out in the Wilderness of Rephaim in his early days as king, preparing to take on the Philistines. He enquires of the Lord as to whether he should go into battle. God says, "Go, for I will certainly hand the Philistines over to you." And he does.

Later, the Philistines come back. Same valley, same battle formation. David asks God whether he should go into battle. Just like Moses and the rock. Same conditions, same need. Last time everything worked out fine. Will David get cocky and assume he knows how to do this? But this time God gives a very different directive for the battle: Attack them from behind, but wait to hear marching in the tops of the trees before you strike. An interesting battle plan to pass onto David's commanders! But here, history does not repeat itself. In this second battle, facing a familiar situation with a non-action plan, David does exactly as God says. This is a crucial test, because like Moses, he is just entering his promise. Because of his commitment to listening and following, David does enter the land as king. He sees all the promises God made to him fulfilled.

And then, once again, he enters a time of testing. When all the promises have been fulfilled . . . what then?

After David has reigned for some years as king, we see a gradual decline from the young man who walked in humility, seeking the face of God for each decision, to an older and more hardened king. Perhaps he has grown complacent. Perhaps he's just tired of the duty of war. For whatever reason, one year when the time comes for him to go out to war, David sends his commander and stays home instead. The story of Bathsheba takes place soon after, with all its ugly details. David takes another man's wife—Bathsheba—and she ends up pregnant. To cover his tracks, he makes sure her husband dies in battle and then marries her. He thinks no one saw what happened. Somehow, he forgets about the One who has seen his whole life to that point.

The story points to keys for our lives. When you have reached the fulfillment of your promise, will the closeness you have cultivated with God continue? Or will he, having served his purpose, be relegated to the outer courts of your life? How many of us (and I must raise my own hand here) ask God for things on a daily basis, receive them, and then forget to even say thank you? The little things are patterns. The bigger life steps will follow in them.

The consequence of David's sin is a promise from God, and this time it's an ugly one: "The sword will never leave your house . . . I am going to bring disaster on you from your own family" (2 Samuel 12:10–11).

As God has been faithful in doing good to David as he followed him wholeheartedly, so God must be faithful to deal with David's sin. We don't like to think about God's justice much, yet God would not be God if he was not completely just. If we will become his friends and walk with him closely, we must understand that we do not have carte blanche to act however we want. Nor does friendship with God immunize us against punishment. David, having destroyed one man's family, stands under sentence to have his own family destroyed from within.

After this incident, David ceases to act decisively in any area of his life. He knows that the full extent of punishment for what he did should have been death. God has been merciful to him in this, though he still bears the consequences. But David ceases to act as a just king, and the kingdom begins to run wild. Perhaps his guilt stares him in the face, preventing him from giving justice to his people and even his family. His sons and army commanders do whatever they wish without fear of punishment. One son rapes a sister and goes unpunished. Another son, Absalom, kills the offender and rushes away into exile. Later David's general convinces David to allow Absalom to return, and this results in Absalom nearly stealing the crown right from under David's nose. Because David does not maintain his authority in the kingdom, it is constantly called into question.

Saddest of all, David seems to cut himself off from God. It is never again recorded that he enquires of the Lord for direction. Oh, sometimes he requests information or asks God to do something for him, but he no longer seeks that inner place of communing with God where God may speak wisdom into a situation. Without the wisdom of God at play, the kingdom shifts and churns, lacking the firm foundation it once had.

It's a scary thing, but a person may abandon God after walking with him for a long time. We all have that option, because God will never take free will from us. But the fall is that much farther. David, by walking with God, became king of Israel. When he sought his own wisdom and way instead of God's, he brought everyone under his authority and protection under the same hardship and judgment.

When you seek the face of God, you do not seek and gain it just for yourself. It is a gift that may be passed down to all those who follow after you. However, if after gaining all this you do not hold it as valuable but treat it with disregard or let it go, your abandonment of God will also affect all those who have gained because of you.

David had an incredible legacy to pass down to his children, but it was truncated halfway through. He was given the promise of an enduring kingdom, and because God is faithful, that promise stood. But David never became the king he could have been. His sons did not have an example to follow when their time came to rule.

The only way to rule an endless kingdom is by following the One who lives forever. Without this crucial piece, the kingdom shatters.

God called David a man "after God's own heart" (1 Samuel 13:14). As the children of God, we carry this lineage and can also be sons and daughters after his heart. But to step into this identity, we must seek his heart and never stop.

MATTHEW

Matthew is not one of Jesus' high-profile disciples. Little is said about him in the gospels, even the one he wrote. He was a tax collector and would not have been popular among his own people. Tax collectors were notorious for being dishonest, so not only had he hired himself out to serve the oppressors of his people, but he was likely getting rich off his own people by overcharging. As far as we can see, before Jesus came along he was not seeking God in any way that made an outward difference in his life.

But the story of his call to follow Jesus is one of the most intriguing in Scripture. Hundreds of years ago, Isaiah referred to people like Matthew:

> I revealed myself to those who did not ask for me; I was found by those who did not seek me. (Isaiah 65:1, NIV)

The human condition is such that we all easily fall into a place of not seeking God. God's surprising response is to show himself even to those who aren't looking. He is a just God: we are each given opportunity to respond to him. This book began by discussing how to win God's attention, but it turns out just the opposite is true. We already *have* God's attention. The door is opened to each person, and the yes or no choice is ours. We will know God as much as we want to know him. We will be as close to him as we wish to be. It all starts with a door of opportunity.

Here was Matthew's:

> As Jesus went on from there, He saw a man named Matthew sitting at the tax office, and He said to him, "Follow Me!" So he got up and followed Him. (Matthew 9:9)

Matthew, behind his tax collector's table, saw the door open in the form of Jesus saying, "Come with me." And he said yes.

Jesus didn't call Matthew because he was worthy of the opportunity. Everyone knew he was a sinner. The religious leaders of the day were offended that Jesus even associated with Matthew and people like him. But Matthew (or Levi, as he was also called) was a little like Abraham. Just like his forefather, when God said "Come follow me," he did it. He didn't question where. He didn't question who. He just went. Here's the story again, this time including the afterparty:

> After this, Jesus went out and saw a tax collector named Levi sitting at the tax office, and He said to him, "Follow Me!" So, leaving everything behind, he got up and began to follow Him.
>
> Then Levi hosted a grand banquet for Him at his house. Now there was a large crowd of tax collectors and others who were guests with

them. But the Pharisees and their scribes were complaining to His disciples, "Why do you eat and drink with tax collectors and sinners?"

Jesus replied to them, "The healthy don't need a doctor, but the sick do. I have not come to call the righteous, but sinners to repentance." (Luke 5:27–32)

The point isn't that we're worthy of God's attention. He isn't choosing us because of our great qualities or what we can offer him. He is choosing us because of the value he has placed on us. He considered the death of his Son to be preferable to eternal separation from us. Think about that for a minute. This has nothing to do with us and everything to do with his love and mercy. It places every person on an equal footing before God. It gives each one an equal chance to become a man or woman after God's heart like David. It gives you just as much chance to be a friend of God as Abraham had, and as I have.

Jesus was calling sinners rather than those who

thought they'd already arrived at righteous status. The Pharisees had no interest in changing. Definitely no interest in a ridiculous call like, "Come follow me." They were much more interested in the finer points of law and righteousness, which they believed pointed out their particular perfections. Engrossed in themselves, they had none of Moses's curiosity and none of David's humility. On the other hand, sinners knew they were sinners. They knew they had a lot to learn. They knew they needed help. These are the people Jesus wanted to be around. The self-proclaimed perfect people he called fancy, painted graves. He promised the eternal kingdom from David's time to the prostitutes and outcasts of society. They were willing to change. And change takes a lot of courage.

When Matthew is called, he embraces radical change. He leaves everything behind—ditches the table, the taxes, the job, the position, the stigma, the routine, and follows Jesus. He can't imagine the journey or the rewards. But because of his yes, he witnesses Jesus' miracles and hears his teaching. He knows Jesus on a daily basis—over the campfire and along the dusty road. His feet are washed by Jesus at the last Passover they share together. He sees the arrest and runs. He hangs around on the outskirts of the place of crucifixion and watches his hopes die a bloody death. And against all hope, he talks to the risen Christ.

None of this is because Matthew sought God. It is because God sought him, and he chose to say yes. Another man in Matthew's neighborhood was given the same offer. Jesus was setting out on a journey, and a man ran up and asked, "Good Teacher, what must I do to inherit eternal life?" After some conversation, Jesus opened the door to relationship:

> Then, looking at him, Jesus loved him and said to him, "You lack one thing: Go, sell all you have and give to the poor, and you will have treasure in heaven. Then come, follow Me." But he was stunned at this demand, and he went away grieving, because he had many possessions. (Mark 10:21–22)

This simple call from God into relationship, though different in its details, was exactly the same invitation given humanity since the beginning of time. But just like everyone else, the young man had a choice. He could have chosen to follow and witness everything Matthew did. He could have heard Jesus teach every day and lived on the road with him. He could have watched a howling storm silenced in a moment. He could have watched the lame walk, the demons run away, and the dead stand up. He could have been at the crucifixion. He could have seen Jesus walk through a locked door and realize he was witnessing a resurrection. He could have been there when the Holy Spirit came down. But he chose his possessions instead—his stuff. The same stuff he would only be able to hang onto for a few years anyway. He traded relationship with Jesus for a few trinkets.

It seems stupid when put that way. But it's so easy for us to put other things before Jesus! Facebook and Netflix call louder than his voice saying, "Come walk with me awhile this evening." When he says, "Go pray for that person," it's simpler to say, "Probably I didn't hear right, and besides, I'm busy with ____."

Jesus does have a way of taking over our whole lives. For the young man who said no, following Jesus would have meant walking away from his wealth and house. It would have been a courageous change. People would have called him crazy. The local rich guy, closing up his house and physically heading down the road in a pair of sandals to live outside with Jesus. Because Jesus *does* call us to live outside. Outside the boundaries created for us. Outside our definition of normal. Outside of the approval of the crowd.

Society has its own values and ways of doing things. To walk with Jesus is to reprioritize our whole lives in a way that's counter to the culture. Sometimes it means you will be misunderstood. You may lose friends. Your life will certainly not look the same as it did before. It will take courage. You will live outside of normal. But what a trade!

The young man would have left business as usual for a life of watching Jesus provide bread and fish out of nowhere, pull the lame to their feet, make mud spitballs to heal the blind, and tell demons just where to get off. But he decided normal life was better.

The interesting thing is, this young man went away sad. His choice, made of his own free will, didn't satisfy him. See, we have the right to choose. But it's never promised that we will live happy, fulfilled lives no matter what we choose. We were made for God—for his love, his companionship, his eternal kingdom. When we choose something else, it's like trying to be satisfied with cardboard instead of food.

So the young man went away sad, back to his cardboard stuff, and we have to wonder what happened to him. Did the sadness and longing get to be too much? Did he choose differently later? (Some suggest this young man may have been Barnabas, companion to the apostle Paul.) Because that's always a possibility for those of us who have said no initially. Or did he just keep on trying to satisfy himself with his wealth? We aren't given the answers. I think that's because in this young man, every one of us can see ourselves. The offer is given, and the price is named. "Give it all up and follow me." The story doesn't say what his permanent choice was, because the question is left there for our lives. Will we go away sad? Or will we find the courage to answer the call, step outside, let them call us crazy, and follow Jesus?

Jesus loved the rich young man. And he loved Matthew. Both were called, and both decided whether to take Jesus up on his invitation. The young man went home. Matthew chose to live outside and see miracles.

JOHN

John, the passionate, intense, uncouth, power-hungry fisherman. His preferred title? *Disciple Jesus loved.* He wrote one of the gospels, but his own name doesn't even show up in the book. His willingness to be transformed is remarkable.

At the beginning, John is very much raw material—one of a set of three fishermen Jesus picks up off the shores of the lake of Galilee. But those three, and particularly John, become closer to Jesus than anyone else. It is a journey and comes with some rough patches, some correction, and some straight-out rebukes. But John's receptivity to everything Jesus says wins his Lord's heart.

We first find John on the job in a fishing boat with his brother James, his friend Peter, and his father Zebedee. A simple call from Jesus has them all scurrying to change their lives. By now we know that a simple yes is a quick way to the heart of God. Their speedy response—immediately up and out of the boat, leaving Zebedee behind with the nets, following Jesus instantly—is definitely a step in the right direction. From this moment, John is all-in as a disciple of Jesus. He takes his allegiance extremely seriously, though sometimes his passion needs some course correction.

Mark the gospel writer remembers John getting upset because he caught someone outside of the in-crowd using Jesus' name to drive out demons. John shuts that rogue behavior down quickly and proudly reports his policing efforts to Jesus. But Jesus' reaction is far from a pat on the back! Jesus lets him know discipleship is not a private club. "Don't stop him," says Jesus, "because there is no one who will perform a miracle in my name who can soon afterward speak evil of me" (Mark 9:39).

John realizes that others will be accepted into Jesus' life just as he has been. He and the others are not the special, exclusive twelve disciples for all time. This journey with Jesus includes a lot more people than he originally guessed.

Years later he writes, speaking of Jesus, "He himself is the propitiation for our sins, and not only for ours, but also for those of the whole world" (1 John 2:2). This is not just about Jesus' closest friends or his wider circle of disciples. It's not even just about the Jews. John realized that the love that was drawing him to Jesus was far bigger than he dreamed. It encompassed the whole world as only the love of God can do.

> Look at how great a love the Father has given us that we should be called God's children.
> (1 John 3:1)

As John comes to see the enormity of God's love, he learns to move from shutting people down to reaching out and including them in that love.

But that's an eventual development. In the story told in the gospels, John still has some lessons to learn.

There's the time the Samaritans don't welcome Jesus, so John and his brother are eager to take revenge into their own hands. Once again, they get a lesson on love. This happens right after James, Peter, and John have been on a mountain with Jesus, seen him transfigured into glowing whiteness before their eyes, and watched him speak with Moses and Elijah. They've had a revelation of his worthiness and power. They're pretty excited about sharing in that worthiness, and especially in that power. So in righteous, self-important indignation against the Samaritans they ask, "Lord, do you want us to call down fire from heaven to consume them?" (Luke 9:54).

Jesus' response is basically that they have no idea what they're talking about. They don't understand his heart for people. He has no problem letting his disciples know they are completely off target: "The

Son of Man did not come to destroy men's lives but to save them." (Luke 9:56, NASB).

Jesus isn't about grabbing what is due him and exercising his right to supremacy. He could do all that in perfect justice, but he chooses to lead gently instead. John is being trained as one of those who will take over the role of gentle shepherd after Jesus leaves. He doesn't know it, but he's being formed into the image of God as he lives in Jesus' presence day after day.

I used to look at the disciples' lives with envy. *If only I could have lived back then,* I'd think. *They had quite the advantage to live with Jesus. No wonder they became such great followers of God!* What I didn't see was that I am the one with the advantage. Doubt it? John heard it right from Jesus: "It is to your advantage that I go away, for if I do not go away, the Helper will not come to you. But if I go, I will send him to you" (John 16:7).

What could be better than living with Jesus? Living with his very Spirit on the inside of us. Jesus was essentially telling them, "I know you think you have it good now, but once I leave it's going to get even better."

> And we all, with unveiled face, beholding the glory of the Lord, are being transformed into the same image from one degree of glory to another. For this comes from the Lord who is the Spirit. (2 Corinthians 3:18, ESV)

With the Spirit of God in us, teaching us at every moment, we're undergoing the same training as those first disciples. We've been chosen by God, but this means the work is only beginning. We have baggage that needs to be left behind: judgment, pride, revenge, fear, greed, and anything else that would put up a barrier between ourselves and the people Jesus is wanting to love through us. He's calling us to have patience with the unlovable. The hostile Samaritans were outcasts as far as the Jews were concerned, yet Jesus wanted to show love and mercy to them. That meant forgiving their unwelcoming attitude and passing by without an angry word. Training for love usually means letting pride go by the wayside.

John gets hold of this at last. One of his letters, many years later, repeats the need for love over and over again:

> Little children, we must not love with word or speech, but with truth and action. (1 John 3:18)

> Now this is his command: that we believe in the name of his Son Jesus Christ, and love one another as he commanded us. (1 John 3:23)

> The one who loves God must also love his brother. (1 John 4:21)

> Dear friends, let us love one another, because love is from God, and everyone who loves has been born of God and knows God. (1 John 4:7)

God is love, and the one who remains in love remains in God, and God remains in him. (1 John 4:16)

But it would be awhile before John got to the point of being able to pen those words.

As time goes on, John is getting hold of the *leader* idea, but he has yet to couple that with the concept of *servant* leadership.

So he and his brother hatch up another great idea. "Teacher, we want you to do something for us if we ask you." Anyone knows there's sure to be trouble when a request for blanket permission comes with no information about the request. My littlest sisters used to try to blindside me on a regular basis. "Shut your eyes for just a minute . . . I have to do something!" It never got them anywhere, but they tried!

Jesus is not easily caught. "What do you want me to do for you?" he asks.

The request is not a small one: "Allow us to sit at your right and at your left in your glory." It's a grasp for an impossibly high position, a bid for power. Jesus recognizes power grabbers when he sees them and turns their angling into a lesson on humility and servanthood.

> Jesus called them over and said to them, "You know that those who are regarded as rulers of the Gentiles dominate them, and their men of high positions exercise power over them. But it must not be like that among you. On the contrary, whoever wants to become great among you must be your servant, and whoever wants to be first among you must be a slave to all. For even the Son of Man did not come to be served, but to serve, and to give His life—a ransom for many." (Mark 10:42–45)

John's immediate response isn't recorded, but later he writes:

> Do not love the world or the things that be-

long to the world. If anyone loves the world, love for the Father is not in him. For everything that belongs to the world—the lust of the flesh, the lust of the eyes, and the pride in one's lifestyle—is not from the Father, but is from the world. And the world with its lust is passing away, but the one who does God's will remains forever. (John 2:15–17)

John came to understand deeply that the point was Jesus. The point was the love of the Father and love for the Father. All the complicated striving for position, the competition and power grabbing, was meaningless and wouldn't last.

John's immediate response to these on-the-ground lessons isn't recorded. But as his life goes on, the fruit becomes evident. It's John who eventually writes, "The one who says he remains in Him should walk just as He walked" (1 John 2:6). John was fully committed to being a disciple of Jesus. Being a disciple means you become like your master. You behave as he does. So as Jesus revealed his character, John brought his own character into line with that. His heart began to change. He began to learn love, starting with Jesus and expanding outward. He began to learn humility and to take on a servant's heart. As his heart was transformed from contact with the heart of God, a deep friendship with Jesus developed.

A few iconic moments show the closeness of their relationship. During the final meal with his disciples, Jesus makes a startling announcement: "One of you will betray me!" This starts a fervor of whisperings and questions around the table, and no one really wants to speak up and ask the obvious question. But John does it. He leans back against Jesus and asks, "Lord, who is it?"

This scene feels familiar. In the midst of trouble or confusing situations, there tends to be a lot of talk. A lot of whisperings and worryings and "what ifs." Wouldn't it be much simpler to first lean back on Jesus and ask the obvious questions? We don't have because we don't ask, as James reminds us.

Sometimes we don't have the answers because we haven't asked the questions. John asks, and Jesus simply answers. Completely straightforward. Not even a parable. "I'll hand this piece of bread to him so you'll know." As simple as that.

Not long after, as Jesus is hanging on the cross, only a few people linger nearby. Most of his disciples have run scared. But a few women, including his mother, are there to his last breath—and so is John. Jesus, as the oldest in his family, is responsible for his mother, and even in his dying moments, he doesn't forget her. Jesus entrusts his mother to his closest disciple, asking them to be family to each other. He asks John to put both lessons into action: love and servanthood. In the midst of his grief, John makes the connection, and he takes Mary into his home from that day onward.

John's changed character stands out towards the end of his gospel. When Jesus' body disappears from the tomb, there's a lot of confusion. Mary Magdalene is crying, Thomas is scoffing, the disciples are locking themselves into hiding in case the Jews come after them next. John doesn't do any of that. When he hears the tomb is empty, he runs to see it for himself. The same love that kept him right beside Jesus to his death is alive and well, and he races to the last place where he saw Jesus' body. When all there is to see is an empty tomb, he takes it all in and just believes. The simple faith that has been carried on by those loved by God since Abraham shows up at daybreak in a garden where a body is missing. Amidst all the ensuing confusion, one man is at peace until Jesus shows up not long after and proves his belief was valid.

John is so much like us. He's got issues, he's got a bit of a messed-up history, and he's sort of bungling his way toward Jesus through all of that. But what matters is that he's moving. He's not sitting back in his fishing boat with his arms crossed, sure that he's got it all together. He's willing to ditch his life as he's known it and walk through the open door, just like Matthew. He's willing to listen and change on the inside. He's willing to be challenged, to be wrong, even to be told off sometimes. He just keeps soaking it all up and correcting his course. He never takes his eyes off Jesus. He's always the disciple trying to get as close as he can to him.

Ultimately, his stumbles don't matter. They pass. He matures. One day, he becomes the one who writes the best-known verse in the Bible, one of piercing simplicity:

> For God so loved the world, that he gave his only Son, that whoever believes in him should not perish but have eternal life. (John 3:16, ESV)

John staked his whole life on that love.

MARY OF BETHANY

Not far from Jerusalem lies the city of Bethany. It's the town where three of Jesus's closest friends lived: Lazarus, Martha, and Mary. They appear several times in the gospels, and the stories about them, while isolated, are most intriguing when read as a continuous story.

We first meet them in Luke 10, just before dinner. Jesus is visiting the three siblings with his disciples and is getting some teaching in while they're waiting for the food to be prepared. The women work in the kitchen, while the men attend to the more important work of study. After all, that's what women do in this culture. They serve the men. That is their place. But then

Mary leaves them and sits down amidst the men.

What causes Mary to do this, to step out of place and sit at Jesus's feet to learn alongside the men, we don't know. What is it she hopes to learn? What is it about Jesus that makes her loath to miss a minute of his visit? Whatever the reason, there she is. Silent, just listening. Absorbing every word he says. Completely forgetting about her kitchen duties and ditching her societal status.

Whatever Jesus was saying to his disciples that day, it's interesting that not a single word of it made it into Scripture. But every child in Sunday School knows what happened because of it. Martha gets irritated with her sister, complains to Jesus about her, and he calmly defies all social convention and lets Mary stay. He says that Mary made the right choice, and he's not about to kick her out to knead bread. Mary doesn't say a thing. After Jesus vindicates Mary, neither does Martha. Luke doesn't even say whether she marches back to the kitchen or sits down beside her sister. The story is open-ended, its conclusion left to our own imaginations and our own decisions.

Where do your sympathies lie? I know I flip-flop between Mary and Martha. At the time of writing, I have a lot to deal with. I help run 1:11 Ministries, doing admin, choreography, costume design, and tour booking. I also work for a small publishing company, teach ballet on the side, and then there's just life—groceries, mowing the lawn, hiring a chimney sweep, the skylight is leaking, and vacuum #3 this year is broken. Also, there's a raccoon in the attic, and there will be insulation in my hair before I oust it. There's a lot to fill my days! Likely there's plenty to keep you busy too. Our culture seems to move faster every year. Stress-related sickness and death are at an all-time high. In the middle of all this, we have to wonder about Jesus's words. What is "the right choice"? What is "the good part" that Mary chose?

All Mary did was sit still and listen to a now-forgotten message. Maybe that's all the "right choice" is, though. Be still in his presence. Sit in front of him and make time for him to speak. Just stop. Stop all the doing. Turn off the phone, close the laptop. Turn off the TV and get quiet. I'm not talking about once or even once in a while. Choose what is good over and over again. We choose good stuff like food and sleep every day. Why do we consider feeding our spirits less necessary than feeding our bodies—when it's our spirits that will exist forever? Let him speak. Let him feed you.

The incident must have had an impact on Mary. Already having made the bold decision to sit and listen with the disciples, she must have questioned herself at her sister's rebuke. Who would Jesus side with? When she received his approval, she must have felt vindicated, special, and loved.

In the quest to come close to God, this is a familiar place. To God we are special. We are absolutely loved. These things are part of our identity, and we can rest in them. But there's a danger here, because favor breeds presumption. "I am special to

God . . . of course he will side with me. He loves me, so how could he deny me what I most need?" Most of us stumble into this ditch on the path to maturity.

So what happens when our Lazarus gets sick? Of course, we confidently pray. After all, God is on our side, and we know that what we need he will hurry to give. We don't see any further than the need in front of us. The job we need to get right now. The illness that surely will be healed right away. The bad things happening to us—they must all be a mistake. Cosmic carelessness. We will remind God to set things right. Except it's not that simple.

Mary's brother Lazarus did get sick, very sick, and when the message is sent—"Lord, the one you love is sick"— Jesus doesn't hurry up and do anything. He stays right where he is for two days. Then he heads to Bethany, but by the time he arrives, it is four days too late for Lazarus. He has died. And Mary has questions. In fact, appearances indicate that she was pretty upset with Jesus. When he arrives, Martha hurries to meet him, but Mary doesn't even get up. She sits in the house. He failed her. Let him come to her and explain. Does he even care?

Now honestly, doesn't this sound familiar? I've certainly done this. I remember being so furious with God once that I refused to talk to him for a month. Self-righteously, I made the excuse that I didn't want to dishonor him with what I might say in anger, but in reality I was just mad. Mad that he had allowed things to happen. Angry that he hadn't fixed it right away. Confused because I was hurt. Hurting people don't tend to think straight, and they push away what will heal them.

John, the writer who recorded this story, approaches it in an unusual way, though. He writes, "Now Jesus loved Martha, her sister, and Lazarus" (John 11:5). In the midst of all the hurt and heartache, John simply states how things were. Jesus loved them. They didn't understand what was going on, but he loved them. They were trying to tell him what to do and reprimanding him when he didn't do it. He still loved them. Even when they sat sulking in the house, he still loved them.

Notice, though, Jesus doesn't meet Mary in the house. He doesn't show up in the place where she is hugging anger and bitterness to herself and try to convince her to talk to him. He calls her out. He is there for her, loves her, and wants to help her. But she has to be willing to be helped. He won't force himself into her world—she has to want him there. It's "come follow me" all over again, even when emotions are billowing in the way.

Again, Mary makes the right choice. She gets up and goes out to him. She's honest about how she feels. "Lord, if you had been here, my brother would not have died!" (John 11:32).

Those are the only words we ever hear Mary speak. "If you had . . . this wouldn't have happened." Translated, she's saying, "You failed me." She thought he loved her, thought she was special, thought he was on her side. All of this was true, but the presumption and expectation that came with all that was wrong.

Mary asks the question so many of us ask: Why? Why does God allow what he allows? Why doesn't he do what we want and think is best? But it's a question that comes out of the pain and mindset of victimhood, and Jesus doesn't tend to meet us there. He didn't for Mary. Instead, he answered with a different question. "Where have you laid him?"

"What have you done with the wreck of your dreams?"

"Where have you hidden your greatest hurt?"

"What is the darkest place of your life?"

With a simple question, Jesus asks Mary to take him to the place of her pain, and it's in this scene that the theory of a distant, emotionless God is debunked. He's described as angry and deeply moved. He's described as crying—weeping. Clearly, he is not emotionally disconnected from Mary's pain.

The author of Hebrews, years later, reinforces this.

> Now since the children have flesh and blood in common, Jesus also shared in these, so that through His death He might destroy the one holding the power of death—that is, the Devil—and free those who were held in slavery all their lives by the fear of death . . . He had to be like His brothers in every way, so that He could become a merciful and faithful high priest in service to God. (Hebrews 2:14–15, 17)

In this moment, Jesus is sharing in the pain of flesh and blood. He's witnessing firsthand the bondage and fear that we experience because of death. As a man, he is sharing their sorrow. As God, he is angry and indignant at the havoc death is wreaking on the human race. Though none of them know it yet, he is preparing both as God and man to die to fully break the power of death.

What happens in the next few moments is a foreshadowing of what is to come. Jesus makes a dead man live. He gives Lazarus back to his sisters in a most unexpected happy ending. (Well, it's possible it was not completely unexpected for Martha—but that's another story.)

For Mary, the resurrection of Lazarus is a wake-up call. She is loved, she is special to Jesus, yes. He will defend her right to be near him, because after all, that's what he did the whole time he was on the earth. He gave the right to be near God to one person after another: to the lepers, the blind, the sick. To the Samaritans, to the women, to the sinners. That's why the temple veil was torn when Jesus died. With his atonement made, the separation between the holiness of God and the sinfulness of man is gone. Anyone can say yes to him and come close. But none of that means that anyone has the right to control him. He is still God; he is still the one calling the shots. As we come close, we can fight against that fact or trust him. It's a choice. We are called to be his, but we still get to make that decision. Ours is a marriage of intimacy and honor, and no close relationship can work without a balance of those two components. Mary understood intimacy. As Lazarus walked out of the tomb, she realized how worthy Jesus was of honor. The final story about her shows the unity of those two attitudes.

Not long after raising Lazarus from the dead, Jesus is back at the house of Mary, Martha, and Lazarus. They're having dinner together with his disciples. We can only imagine what the conversation would have been like. After all, one of the men enjoying dinner spent four days dead in a grave not long ago. Another of them walked up to his tomb and told him to come on out, so he did. Their recent history is all a little overwhelming.

Then there's Mary, who has clearly been doing some thinking. There is no doubt left in her mind as to who Jesus is: God himself. How do you deal with God at your dinner table? How do you deal with the fact that you were angry and disappointed in him a few days ago, and he didn't retaliate but raised your dead brother to life again? Awe, embarrassment, gratitude, fear, and confusion must have been among the many emotions that fought within her. Ultimately, love wins out. She remembers how he defended her as she sat at his feet. She remembers how he first shared and then healed her sorrow. And as she remembers these things, intimacy and honour come together in a beautiful act of devotion.

The story is told briefly: "Then Mary took a pound of fragrant oil—pure and expensive nard—anointed Jesus' feet, and wiped His feet with her hair. So the house was filled with the fragrance of the oil" (John 12:3).

The cost of the oil is about a year's wages: tens of thousands of dollars in today's world. Imagine giving a gift like that over supper. Not at all conventional. Not only that, but for Mary there are further societal issues. Women do not uncover their hair in public. This is not at all socially acceptable behaviour, yet Mary does it. Not only that, but Jesus lets her do it. Apparently he isn't hung up on societal norms. She is bringing the best of what she has to offer, and she is bringing it out of love. She is putting herself at his feet, as a servant, to honor him. And she is confident that as before, he will accept her presence because he loves her back. To her, that was all that mattered.

She is right: Jesus accepts her gift and the honor she shows him. Of course, there's some muttering, most notably from Judas, who is irritated at the sight of all that money going to waste. Considering that he generally helps himself to what is given to Jesus, he's irked that this time he has no chance of getting a cut. Once again, Jesus defends her. "Leave her alone," he says. "You do not always have me here."

Mary has recognized Jesus for who he is: Emmanuel, God with us. In this moment, while God is physically present at her dinner table, she will bring everything she has and offer it in love, honor, and gratitude. It's the final "thank you" just before he goes to the cross. The final "I believe"—a firstfruit of the many others who believe. And a final, simple, "I love you." Her understanding of how to unite intimacy with honor wins the heart of God.

MY STORY

Throughout Scripture, we read the record of those who interacted with God and had unexpected, incredible encounters. I've covered a few in this book, but there are many more. Noah, who was directed to build a gigantic boat to save a remnant of humanity and creation. Joshua, who lost all fear after prolonged time spent in the presence of God. Samuel, who talked with God as a child. Enoch, who simply walked with him—all the way to heaven. Elijah, who cured lepers, denounced kings, and scoffed at false prophets. Nehemiah, who rebuilt dead cities. Paul, who was struck blind so he could see for real. Peter, who walked on water and through prison gates.

The list goes on throughout the Scriptures . . . but it goes on after that too. It goes on with every single person who has ever said yes to God since the end of Revelation was penned. Martin Luther, who dared to challenge the way everything had "always" been done. William Tyndale, who had the crazy idea that everyone should be able to access the Word of God for themselves. Count Zinzendorf, who broke church barriers between slaves and nobility because he believed we are all one in Christ. Nate Saint, who braved jungle wilderness to reach those who had never heard of Jesus.

But it's not just the big names that count. The stories continue with the missionaries, the farmers, the pastors, the grocers, the orphans in the streets, the kings, the mystics, the beggars, the revivalists, and every other curious, hopeful soul who has ever sought God out. No matter their station in life. He never seems to care what or who they were in the world's eyes or even their own, because he knows who he sees them as and what they can become through him.

A beggar can become a prince in God's kingdom. A shopkeeper can walk with God. A king can become a child of God. Anyone who seeks an encounter with God is changed to the core of their identity. The lineage of those who walk with God continues today. The stories of connection are yours and mine as well.

Let me tell you mine.

My grandfather was a pastor. When I was born, my father was also a pastor. One of my earliest memories is saying yes to God when I was three years old. Now, a three-year-old doesn't know much, but I did know I meant what I said. It wasn't so long after saying yes that I started to wonder how to get God's attention, because I thought I'd like him and I wanted to find out. I wanted to try out what my mom had called "flirting," which I thought was just a fancy term for getting someone's attention. I wanted him to talk to me. I had a lot of questions. So many in fact, that one day at about age five I asked God to please write them all down on a big scroll so when I'd get to heaven, I could ask them all. I was worried I might forget a few before I got there. "And write them in gold, please," I requested. "Because I know you're quite rich, so that won't be a problem." It didn't occur to me at the time that I could just ask the question and see if he answered right then. So I let him know with the simple audaciousness of a child that I wanted his opinion on things, and someday when I could see and hear him, I knew he'd explain it all.

By seven, my theories about heaven and gold scrolls were toppling a bit. For one thing, God was talking to me. He wasn't answering all those questions, because I wasn't listening for those answers just then. But he'd heard my hopeful "I wish you'd talk to me," so he did. I would swing on the white gate in the backyard, and he'd talk to me about stuff that most people would consider far too hefty for a kid. Politics and cultural attitudes and societal problems and what he thought about it and what he was going to do about it. I chimed in with my opinions anytime I thought I might be helpful. I was a child. Audacious, like I said. I guess he liked it.

By eleven or twelve, I was pretty addicted. I was growing up in a big family (six siblings at the time), and I loved being with them all. But my favorite time was after everyone, including myself, was packed off to bed. It was the only time I was alone, and sometimes I could hardly wait for evening. I knew he'd come once I could pay attention to him, and his presence filling the room was what I craved as I fell asleep.

But it was when I was nineteen that something big happened. It started with a question. Probably one I had asked at five. I hadn't run around and gotten into trouble in my teen years. I'd lived a steady, busy life pursuing education, helping with my now seven siblings, and trying to be persistent in reading a Bible that I really felt I knew all about by this point. At the same time, it frustrated me, because I knew I couldn't possibly know everything about the Bible or about God. But it was same-old by this point. So I asked.

"God. If there's more to you than what I know right now, I'd like to know about it."

That was all. I wasn't asking out of doubt. I knew there was more. But I stuck the "if" in just to let him know I was a bit frustrated, the ball was in his court, and I was curious.

Of course, he answered. It wasn't how I expected. I don't really know what I expected—maybe a little more Bible study insight, greater motivation to pray . . . something nice and normal like that.

His idea was to walk into my room one night. I can't explain it to this day. But there was no question that he was there and he was very big. I did what anyone else would do if God showed up in their house. Gaped, worshipped, and didn't fall asleep until about 3 a.m. I hadn't known he was like that.

Shortly after I fell asleep, I heard someone call my name, and I sat up and answered. I'd trained myself pretty well to keep a sleeping ear open for little sisters who might need me in the wee hours.

Or maybe it was the friend who was staying over and had experienced the same incredible encounter along with me. But it wasn't my friend, and it wasn't a little sister. The voice that had awakened me was God's. To this point, that's the only time I've heard him audibly. But he woke me up just to say firmly, "I will be with you."

And he was. In the month that followed I was far more aware of the spiritual world than the physical one. It was not uncommon to be aware of angels in the room. Sometimes I saw demons, but even though that was terrifying, they were always pathetic too—and even a bit silly-looking beside the glory of God. And he was always, always there, just like he said he would be.

I had no box for this kind of experience and no one to explain it to me but him. All of a sudden I discovered I could ask any question and hear what he thought about it. We talked for hours.

In the "real world," this caused some problems. I gained a reputation for being far too quiet—some people even thought depressed, or in need of an attitude adjustment to make the switch back to what I used to be. I suppose it did seem like a pretty big mood swing! But the truth was, I was just quiet. I didn't want to miss a thing God might have to say. Those who knew me were right; for a time I had zoned out of "normal life." But what was going on around and through the borders of normal life was more than a little distracting.

I gained two new favorite occupations. First, the Bible became alive. I read it like it was the first time and talked about it with God at great length. He had a lot to say about it, and I was eager to listen.

Second, I learned what worship was. I loved to sneak downstairs to a quiet room, turn on worship music, and get lost for hours. He was so worthy of worship, and I loved giving it to him. I also loved seeing others worship him, whether it was within a church context or simply the angelic beings that always crowded the room to join the worship in those evenings.

None of this was because I was a great spiritual person. It was simply a "what else do you do?" response to the external events taking place around me. It was complete culture shock, and I embraced it clumsily, confusedly, sometimes scared, but wholehearted. The more I ran into the encounter, the more I discovered his joy in running with me. I discovered his incredible Father-heart. I discovered I was this incredible being called "Beloved"—not because of anything I had achieved or could hope to earn. Simply because it was his delight to love me passionately. And I learned that his Spirit in me could make the whole world and every person in it look different, because I could see with his eyes and process with his mind.

I've often wondered why my simple request led to such a crazy, prolonged encounter. But it ensured one thing at least. I knew God truly was far bigger than I'd thought, I was all his, and there was no going back. And that was important, because there would certainly be pressure to do so.

After the first month, the constant visions lessened. His presence did not. We still talked continually, and I was more in love with him every day.

In the practical world, I got very busy. That year, my days ran from 4 a.m. to 11 p.m., and I was often half-asleep on my feet. What I had gone through in the last month had changed me, and the outcome of that was sometimes tough to deal with. I tried to explain it to people, though I suspect I didn't do a terribly good job. I didn't know how to do "normal" anymore, and the resultant miscommunication, accusations, and disapproval were hard to deal with. For whatever reason, I didn't ask God how to deal with it. I simply asked him to make it stop. When he didn't, I got scared. Because I wasn't asking the right questions, I ran into a blind alley. (For the record, "What are you doing?" is always a good question!)

So I had a few silent years. I was stuck in a quandary of wanting to be acceptable to people on the outside but knowing I had been massively changed on the inside. Eventually I took the easy way. I wouldn't let go of the inner change; in fact, I was determined to pursue it secretly as much as I could. But I learned that silence and self-effacement were safe, for the most part. It was hard, but I thought perhaps God was trying to work on my character (which, in part, he was), so I tried to cooperate as best I knew how.

So all those years, I never talked to anyone about what had happened. I never processed or learned what to do with it all in the context of a church body. Sometimes I wondered about some of it. Especially about being loved so much. I still talked with him, but I felt very isolated and wondered if he really meant the bit about being loved beyond all comprehension. Maybe that part had been my imagination . . . it really was a bit much to believe.

Then one day, I met someone who did not give in to my stand-off-don't-touch-me-I'm-an-ice-princess vibe. She seemed to want to get past my thick, self-protective walls and hear my heart. After seven years, I didn't even know how to let her in. I was caught firmly in the trap of "I love God and I'll tell people about him, but I won't let them get close to me." But she was very persistent, and slowly I began telling my story. Expecting at every moment to be rejected. Waiting for the raised eyebrow, the polite nod, or the flat-out "You're crazy." It never came. As I revisited those memories, I found them strengthened by her companionship and acceptance. This was entirely new. With that encounter, I began the path back into the body of Christ—the church.

One night I began to wonder about my doubts. I was sitting outside with God, and we were starwatching. "You know," I started, "I thought you said some stuff about love a long time ago. And I really don't know now if that was just me, or if it was you and you really meant it. But I've never forgotten, and I wish you'd tell me. I'm willing to be wrong. I'd just like to know one way or another."

He smiled. "Tomorrow, you will know," he said. And that was all I could get out of him that night.

The next day, a woman I had never seen came up to me with her eyes big. "Please, can I tell you what God has shown me about you?"

Now that pushed every button I had. First, I had major trust issues with people, and second, I knew enough not to believe everyone who thought they had a word from the Lord. And most importantly, I didn't fully trust him. I had known so much hurt and tried to bear it all to hopefully shape my character, and it didn't seem unlikely that the next thing he might do would be send someone who would see my inmost self and come with an accompanying rebuke. (Of course, that was not his view of it, but I wasn't seeing straight at the time.) I was scared, because somehow I knew in that moment that she was no phony. The rebuke when it came would be deserved, whatever it might be. But then I stopped in my tracks. She had asked permission. *He* had asked permission. He had something he wanted to say to me, and here he was not pushing his way into my hurting heart but standing there quietly asking permission to speak. Trust began to flicker back to life. I said yes.

The words she spoke were identical to what he had said to me about love seven years earlier. The words that identified me as Beloved. He hadn't forgotten. He had really meant it.

That day, I took back my identity. No matter what anyone says, no matter who doubts it, I know who I am. I am loved beyond comprehension. I am loved in every crazy, beyond-belief, undeserved way that his love is found in the pages of Scripture and within his own heart. I am Beloved of the Lord, and nothing can touch that.

In the years since that day, there have been hard times and situations that have tried to shake me. But I walk in this identity as securely as I walk in the knowledge that he walked into my room one night and called me by name. He wants to talk with me, as I could not have imagined as a five-year-old requesting golden scrolls. Our friendship and love is one that will deepen through my life and after. I am deeply content and still insatiably curious.

YOUR STORY

Everyone has a different story with God. For some it's big and dramatic; for others it's a slow, sure climb. Some go on to change the world. Others change their communities. Some simply love the handful that are close to them. It's tempting to point the finger and say, "This person is great . . . this one not so much." But before we start judging with our limited vision of just a few years on earth, let's get an eternal perspective. Here's what Paul, one of the first missionaries, had to say:

> This is how one should regard us, as servants of Christ and stewards of the mysteries of God. Moreover, it is required of stewards that

they be found faithful. But with me it is a very small thing that I should be judged by you or by any human court. In fact, I do not even judge myself. For I am not aware of anything against myself, but I am not thereby acquitted. It is the Lord who judges me. Therefore do not pronounce judgment before the time, before the Lord comes, who will bring to light the things now hidden in darkness and will disclose the purposes of the heart. Then each one will receive his commendation from God. (1 Corinthians 4:1–5, ESV)

The point is not "big" or "small" by human standards. The point is the purposes of the heart—how the deepest inside part of you stands in relation to God. The point is the commendation—the praise—you will receive from God.

There have been times when I felt judged by people and was so confused I couldn't even judge the situation myself. In those times, this concept has been my consolation. What matters is how I am seen by God. Not how I am seen by others. Not what I think of myself. The point is to keep my heart open to him and be ready to do as he says in any area. When we walk in this way, whether in hard or easy circumstances, we can be secure in his judgment. It will always be fair.

Everyone wants their life to have some meaning, and this is the answer to that desire: Be as he is calling you to be, however strange it may seem. Big or small doesn't matter.

The whole point is found in a little book by an Old Testament prophet that tells us what God is looking for:

> The LORD has told us what is good. What he requires of us is this: to do what is just, to show constant love, and to live in humble fellowship with our God. (Micah 6:8, GNT)

That's all. Do what's right. Act according to his heart. Love and don't stop. Just like he does. And finally, as some translations say, "walk" with God.

Day in, day out, in the mundane like Abraham. Invite him into your space. Looking for more of him like Moses. Humbly, as David did. Watching for the open doors and running through them like Matthew. Stumbling, perhaps, but always grabbing hold of the lessons as John the Beloved did. Like Mary, never putting your own hurt in the way of the love between you.

That's how a story is written. But a story was also meant to be told. Jesus said to go preach the good news through the whole earth. The good news is what he has done for humanity, but often the open door to share that huge story with others is to share what he has done for you. This is how Jesus taught evangelism. One of the first missionaries Jesus ever sent out was a man who had been filled with demons just a short time before. Jesus cast them all out and restored the man's sanity to him. Of course, the man begged to be allowed to go with Jesus after this. But Jesus said, "'Go back to your home, and tell all that God has done for you.' And off he went, proclaiming throughout the town all that Jesus had done for him" (Luke 8:39).

The man had a story of mercy, grace, and redemption, and Jesus wanted him to tell it. Such a story would certainly spread and send curious seekers looking for Jesus. Did the man have it all together yet? Certainly not. But he could offer a starting point. That was all Jesus asked of him.

What will your story be?

Oh, you have one. Or you will, in a minute. It starts with a question. Not yours. His. He's already asked. "Will you come?"

You just have to say yes.

The hard part may come after the yes, because we realize we've stepped into something bigger than we are and we're no longer in control. We want to take hold of the situation, make it something, justify our yes in a way that's palatable to us and to others. Don't do it. Just let your yes stand and see what God does with it. He won't ignore it. This is a relationship, after all. The two of you are in this together, and the ball goes back and forth. Your yes throws him the ball. Your story begins as he throws it back.

Your story has life-changing value. Go live it. Go tell it.

1:11 MINISTRIES
WORD. DANCE. MUSIC.

Live productions, events, and books
to inspire and empower the body of Christ.

*Learn how you can bring Carolyn and the 1:11 Ministries
team to your church, conference or event at:*

one11ministries.com

FEARLESS

You can live free from fear.

Fear steals our lives from us. It steals our impact and cripples our joy.

In our modern world, there are a million reasons to be afraid.

But what if your default mode was courage and faith, not fear and timidity?

True freedom is possible—through the presence of Jesus and the practice of his Word.

In this book, we expose the insidious roots of fear and explore the answers found in the Bible. Learn how:

- THE FEAR OF THE LORD WILL BREAK THE POWER OF LESSER FEARS

- HOLINESS WILL CHANGE YOUR IDENTITY—AND GIVE YOU COURAGE TO STAND AGAINST THE TIDE

- THE PRESENCE OF GOD IS THE ANSWER TO THE WORLD'S TROUBLES

- YOU CAN PRACTICE THE GIFTS OF POWER, LOVE, AND A SOUND MIND

Available from Amazon and everywhere books are sold.

TIME TO ALIGN:
FREE EMAIL COURSE

Join Carolyn Currey and the 1:11 team for a personal journey through 8 key areas of life in our free email-based course, "Time to Align."

This free, 11-week course is a spiritual recalibration: a chance to bring your heart, soul, mind, and strength into alignment with the nature and will of God.

To get your first lesson straight to your inbox, sign up here:

One11Ministries.com/Align

www.ingramcontent.com/pod-product-compliance
Lightning Source LLC
Chambersburg PA
CBHW021154080526
44588CB00008B/330